CW00853298

Paleo
Slow Cooker Meals

45 Easy Nutrient-Rich Recipes

By

Patrick Smith

ISBN-10: 1500383309
ISBN-13: 978-1500383305

Contents

Introduction: The Paleo Diet

"Paleo" refers to the "Paleolithic era", otherwise known as the "Stone Age", in which mankind lived in the wild, ate natural foods that were available and weren't grown or otherwise produced.

We know that peoples and tribes that still live in this manner are unusually healthy. For example, the Tokelauan people and their neighbors, who live on islands in the South Pacific, get most of their daily calories from coconuts.

Coconuts are extremely rich in "good" saturated fatty acids. In consequence, the Tokelauans consume more saturated fats than anyone else in the world – even more than an obese American. However, they are built like Olympic athletes. Heart disease, diabetes, depression and other modern diseases of civilization are unheard of among them.

The secret of their health is the natural foods they eat. We also know this to be true for Eskimos, even though they eat whale, which is very rich in fat as well.

Aligning with these results, the paleo diet wants you to eat natural foods, such as fish, organic meat produced from free ranging cows, coconut products and so on. On the other hand, it doesn't want you to eat beans, peas, dairy products or grains, which means no noodles, no bread and a lot of other foods.

The real problems to our health are processed foods, the chemicals and so called trans fats that are being used or created in these processes. We know today that trans fats are what cause heart disease, because they clog arteries. In fact, at the end of 2013, the US Food and Drug Administration decided to ban trans fats, so they are going to be weeded out of the foods in America, an enormous victory for medical science that has been fighting for this for decades. It is likely the rest of the world will follow this example in time.

To be paleo, all foods must be organic. This is especially critical when it comes to meat.

Ordinary meat comes from cattle raised on corn instead of grass. To produce this meat, the animals are first pumped full of growth hormones to make them insanely hungry, because otherwise they won't eat the corn. They instinctively know their stomach isn't built for this kind of food, but with the hormone-induced hunger, they are driven to eat it. The corn turns their stomach so acidic that it becomes a seething cauldron of bacterial growth. Now the cow has to be pumped full of antibiotics to ensure it won't die of an infection.

That mess is what you consume, if you don't go for organic meat. Why do we do this to our cows, you ask? It makes them grow really fast, so a farmer can sell more meat per month. Organic meat is more expensive, because the farmers that produce it have less to sell and need to raise the price to compensate.

Not all people choose a 100% paleo lifestyle and wish to supplement with some non-paleo ingredients. This choice is perfectly fine, because we have some healthy foods today that simply were not available to people in the Stone Age.

If you choose to live semi-paleo, go for whole-grains, be it rice, noodles or bread. Never go for white noodles, white rice or white bread. These are not whole-grain and have almost no nutritional value. White bread in particular is so empty, it turns into a doe like paste in your stomach. It is only something to fill yourself with so the hunger goes away, but gives your body nothing to work with. You can also go for occasional beans and peas, since they are great sources of iron.

Now, let's start cooking!

Patrick Smith

Section 1: Paleo Food Replacements

Since rice, noodles and potatoes are not paleo, we need to use alternatives.

The standard paleo replacement for rice is **cauliflower rice**. It is made entirely from cauliflower and simulates rice much better than most people think before they try it.

The only type of potato that works with the paleo diet are **sweet potatoes**. Simply use them instead of other potato types.

For noodles, you can either make egg noodles with **almond flour** or **coconut flour** instead if regular flour, or you can slice **Zucchinis** into noodle shapes.

In this section, I explain how to make the rice and Zucchini noodles.

1. Paleo Cauliflower Rice

Cauliflower rice is the standard paleo replacement for regular rice. As the name suggests, it is made entirely from cauliflower.

30 oz. (850 g) **cauliflower** (chopped coarsely)
1 **onion** (chopped finely)
1 ½ tbs **coconut oil**
2 tbs **coconut butter**
Salt and **pepper**

Makes 6 servings
Calories: 40 per serving

Remove leaves and discolored parts from the cauliflower, then chop into chunks. Place in a food processor and hack until the parts are the size of regular rice grains.

Heat the coconut butter and coconut oil in a skillet and sauté the onions until translucent. Add the cauliflower rice and distribute evenly.

Season the mix with salt and pepper or other seasonings of your choice.

Cover and cook for 7-10 minutes.

2. Paleo Zucchini Noodles

There are two ways to replace pasta that I use myself.

One way is to use almond flour or coconut flour instead of regular flour and make grain-free paleo noodles from scratch.

Another way is to turn Zucchinis into spaghetti, which is quick and easy.

6 **Zucchinis**
Salt and **pepper**

Makes 4 servings
Calories: 38 per serving

There is an easy and a slightly harder way to do this.

The harder way is to use a julienne peeler to cut the Zucchinis into slices.

The easy way is to use a spiral slicer, which you probably have to buy first. You can find them on Amazon.

Fry the noodles in a skillet using coconut oil, or microwave them on a high setting for 2-3 minutes.

Section 2: Main Dishes

1. Barbecue Chicken

This is a tangy and sweet barbeque chicken. It goes well with sweet potatoes or cauliflower rice, which is no grain and suitable for the paleo diet.

24 oz. (680 g) **boneless chicken breast**
¼ cup **Italian dressing**
1 tbs **Worcestershire sauce**
2 tbs **chicken broth**
¾ cup organic **barbeque sauce**
2 tbs **arrowroot flour** or **coconut flour**

Makes 8 servings
Calories: 170 per serving

Place the chicken at the bottom of the slow cooker. Mix the dressing, barbeque sauce and Worcestershire sauce in a container, then stir to combine.

Pour over the chicken and cook for 5 hours on low heat.

Remove the chicken and set aside on a cutting board to cool for a few minutes. Shred the chicken into pieces.

Combine the flour of your choice and chicken broth in a bowl. Slowly add into the sauce and cover until it is thick and heated through.

Return the chicken and continue to cook for another 45 minutes.

Enjoy!

2. Family Chilaquiles

Chilaquiles is a Mexican favorite that combines cilantro, chipotle and chicken. There are many ways to prepare Chilaquiles. This one is less traditional, but a family favorite.

The paleo tortillas used in this recipe are explained in recipe 9a.

4 **chicken breasts**
1 ¼ cups **red bell pepper** (shredded)
¾ cup **chicken broth**
1 tbs **cumin** (ground)
6 **garlic cloves**
4 oz. (110 g) **green chilies** (chopped)
2/3 cup **queso fresco** (crumbled)
1 ½ cup **red onion** (chopped)
1 ¼ cups **green bell pepper** (chopped)
¼ cup fresh **cilantro**
2 tbs **chili** (chopped)
50 oz. (1.4 kg) **tomatoes** (roasted)
5 cups **paleo tortillas** from recipe 9a

Makes 10 servings
Calories: 220 per serving

Follow recipe 9a to make the paleo tortillas.

Heat a large pan over medium heat. Place the chicken at the bottom, then cook for 3 to 4 minutes on each side. Cook until golden brown.

Mix the onion, red bell pepper, green bell pepper, low sodium chicken broth, fresh cilantro, cumin, chipotle, garlic cloves, tomatoes and green chilies. Place the mix in a slow cooker.

Remove the chicken from the pan and transfer it to the cooker. Cover and cook for 4 hours on medium heat.

Remove the chicken from the slow cooker and the meat from the bones. Return the chicken into the soup.

Divide into bowls and ladle the soup over the paleo tortillas.

Enjoy!

3. Mediterranean Chicken Meal

Mediterranean recipes are often dominated by ingredients such as lemon, olives and tomatoes. Serve this dish with mashed sweet potatoes. Remember to use organic meat.

1 **lemon**
¼ cup **olives**
15 oz. (425 g) **plum tomatoes** (roughly chopped)
¼ tsp **black pepper** (ground)
¾ cup **onion** (chopped)
2 tbs **drained capers**
12 bone in **chicken thighs**
1 tbs **olive oil** or **coconut oil**
Rosemary (optional, chopped)
Fresh parsley (optional, chopped)

Makes 6 servings
Calories: 215 per serving

Grate the lemon to get 1 tbs of zest. Also, squeeze the lemon to get 1 tbs of juice. Combine the zest and juice in a bowl. Cover and refrigerate.

Combine the onion, lemon juice, olives, drained capers and plum tomatoes in a slow cooker. Season the chicken thighs with pepper.

Heat the oil of your choice in a pan over medium heat. Place the chicken thighs in a pan, then cook for 3 minutes on each side until brown.

Add the chicken thighs to the slow cooker. Cook for 4 hours on medium heat until brown and tender.

Place the chicken on plates and stir in the lemon sauce.

Garnish with desired amount of rosemary and parsley.

4. Apple Chicken

This recipe is rich in taste. It combines chicken, apples and herbs and produces a delicious smell in your house.

2 lb. (900 g) **chicken breasts** (boneless, skinless)
2 **apples** (cored, sliced)
2 **garlic cloves** (smashed)
1 **bay leaf**
2/3 cups **chicken broth**
1 **onion** (sliced)
2 tbs **ginger** (grated)
1 tsp **cinnamon**
½ tsp **paprika**
1 tsp **salt**
1/2 tsp **pepper**

Makes 15 servings
Calories: 270 per serving

Combine the chicken broth, onions and chicken breasts in a slow cooker.

Add the apples on top and sprinkle with the spices, then top with the bay leaf.

Cover and set to low heat. Cook for 9 hours.

Remove and shred the chicken. This dish goes well with roasted sweet potatoes.

Enjoy!

5. Stuffed Bell Peppers

This is a quick and easy dish that you can prepare in just 15 minutes and leave for 4 hours.

¾ cup **water**
8 oz. (225 g) organic **spicy sausage**
¼ tsp **pepper** (ground)
4 **small red bell peppers**
½ cup **cauliflower rice** (see section 1)
1/8 tbs **salt**
½ cup **garlic**
½ cup **coconut cream**
2 tbs **basil** (sliced)

Makes 4 servings
Calories: 305 per serving

Bring the water to a boil in a small pan. Stir in cauliflower rice, then remove from heat. Cover and set aside for 5 minutes.

Remove the casing from the sausage and cook in a pan over medium heat for 5 until it is done. Stir to crumble. Remove from heat and set aside.

Add the salt and pepper. Stir in the coconut cream.

Cut the tops of the bell peppers and remove seeds and flesh inside. Sprinkle with salt and scoop the sausage mixture into the peppers. Return the pepper tops.

Place the stuffed peppers in a slow cooker, set to low heat and cook for 4 hours or until tender. Garnish the pepper with basil and coconut cream if desired.

Enjoy!

6. Chicken Thighs with Tomato and Olives

12 **chicken thighs**
¼ tsp **black pepper** (ground)
1 ½ tbs **garlic** (minced)
3 tbs **tomato paste**
28 oz. (800 g) **tomatoes** (diced)
2 tbs **flat leaf parsley** (chopped)
1 tsp **salt**
1 tsp **olive oil**
3 tbs **crushed red pepper**
¼ cup **olives** (pitted)

Makes 6 servings
Calories: 250 per serving

Season the chicken with salt and pepper. Heat the oil in a pan and sauté the chicken for 2 minutes on each side until browned.

Place the chicken inside the slow cooker and add garlic, then stir occasionally. Scrape the bottom of the pan to remove browned bits. Continue to sauté for 30 seconds.

Add the red pepper, tomato paste and tomatoes. Cover, set heat to high and cook for 4 hours.

If desired, add more parsley, olives and seasoning for more flavors. Add the parsley last.

Enjoy!

7. Chicken Drummettes with Dip

Chicken drummettes are a classic favorite and can be served with vegetables, cauliflower rice or mashed sweet potato. This recipe contains the option to include some vinegar, which is a "gray ingredient" in the paleo diet and has been adopted by many that follow a paleo lifestyle.

48 oz. (1.36 kg) **chicken wing drums** (skinned)
¾ cup paleo **hot sauce**
1 tsp low-salt **Worcestershire sauce**
Coconut cream (as dip)
28 **carrots**
¼ tsp **black pepper** (ground)
2 tbs **balsamic vinegar** (optional)
2 **garlic cloves** (minced)
28 **celery sticks**

Makes 14 servings
Calories: 100 per serving

Preheat the oven to 450F (230°C). Place foil at the bottom of a jelly roll pan. Coat the foil with cooking spray. Put the chicken in the pan and sprinkle with pepper. Coat the chicken with cooking spray, then bake for 7 minutes until brown.

Combine the hot sauce, optional vinegar, Worcestershire sauce and garlic cloves in a slow cooker.

Remove the chicken from the pot, then drain the excess oil. Put the chicken in the slow cooker and coat with sauce. Cover and cook for 3 hours on high heat or until the chicken is tender.

Serve with carrots sticks, celery sticks and coconut cream as dip.

Enjoy!

8. Spicy Mushrooms

If this recipe included black beans instead of mushrooms and cauliflower rice, it could be a Mexican dish. In case you are wondering, the pumpkin seeds are indeed a paleo ingredient.

8 oz. (225 g) **mushrooms**
8 oz. (225 g) **cauliflower rice**
2 cups **onion** (chopped)
1 tsp **salt**
1 tbs **lime juice**
½ cup fresh **cilantro** (chopped)
3 cups (700 ml) **chicken broth**
1 tbs **chipotle chili** (chopped)
4 **garlic cloves** (minced)
4 oz. (110 g) **coconut cream** (optional)
½ cup **pumpkin seeds** (not salted)

Makes 14 servings
Calories: 160 per serving

Place the mushrooms and cauliflower rice in a Dutch oven and pour water until it covers the ingredients for about 2 inches (5 cm). Cook for 2 minutes on high heat. Remove and allow to cool for an hour, then drain.

Place the mixture in a slow cooker. Stir in the broth, chopped onion, chipotle, salt, and garlic cloves. Cover and cook for 8 hours in low heat.

Add the lime juice and mash the mixture until it is soft and thick. Top with the pumpkin seeds, cilantro and optional coconut cream.

Enjoy!

9a. Paleo Tortillas

Some of the recipes in this book require tortillas. This means you either need to buy paleo tortillas somewhere or make them yourself. Here's how to do it.

4 **eggs**
2 tsp **coconut oil** (melted)
½ cup **arrowroot powder**
2 tsp **coconut flour**
2 pinches of **salt**
½ tsp **vanilla extract** (optional)

Makes six 8 inch (20 cm) tortillas
Calories: 65 per tortilla

Crack the eggs and pour into a bowl. Add the melted coconut oil and whisk.

Add coconut flour, arrowroot powder and salt. Beat well to combine.

Put a skillet over medium heat. Add 1/6 of the tortilla batter and quickly coat the bottom evenly.

Cook for 1 minute on each side. Repeat until six tortillas are made.

After the tortillas are done, they can be stored in an airtight plastic bag or glass container. Let them cool first.

Enjoy!

9b. Stacked Chicken Enchilada

This recipe uses the paleo tortillas from recipe 9a. As always, choose organic meat.

1 tsp **olive oil** or **coconut oil**
½ cup **poblano chili** (chopped)
1 ½ tsp **chipotle chili powder**
8 oz. (225 g) **tomato sauce with garlic, oregano and basil**
2 cups **chicken breast** (shredded)
15 oz. (425 g) **mushrooms**
1 cup **onion** (chopped)
2 **garlic cloves** (minced)
14 oz. (400 g) **tomatoes** (unsalted, diced)
Cooking spray
1 cup **cauliflower rice**
5 **paleo tortillas** from recipe 9a

Makes 9 servings
Calories: 290 per serving

Heat a large pan in medium heat. Add oil in a pan then swirl to coat. Add the chili, garlic and onion in the pan, then sauté for 6 minutes until the vegetables are tender. Stir in the tomato sauce, tomatoes and chili powder.

Place the tomato mixture in a blender and allow steam to escape by removing the center lid. Place a towel at the opening to prevent spills. Blend until smooth. Pour the mixture in a large bowl. Repeat procedure until the tomato mixture is well blended.

Coat the cooker with cooking spray. Place 3 tbs of tomato mixture in a bowl, then add the cauliflower rice, chicken and mushrooms. Place a paleo tortilla in the slow cooker, then pour the chicken mixture. Top with another tortilla. Continue to layer the chicken and tomato mixture in this way. Cook for 2 hours on low heat. Cut into pieces and serve.

10. Satsuma Turkey

The oranges and marmalade provides a sweet and tangy flavor, while the pepper adds a spicy kick to the dish. As always, choose organic meat.

3 cups **red onions** (thinly sliced)
2/3 cup fresh **orange juice**
2 tsp **tamarind paste**
60 oz. (1.7 kg) bone-in **turkey thighs** (skinned)
1 tsp **salt**
2 cups fresh **mandarin orange** (sectioned)
1/3 cup **orange marmalade**
½ tsp **red pepper** (crushed)
2 tsp **five spice powder**
1 tbs **olive oil** or **coconut oil**
1 ½ tbs **arrowroot flour** or **coconut flour**

Makes 8 servings
Calories: 280 per serving

Combine the red onions, orange juice, marmalade, tamarind paste and red pepper in a slow cooker.

Rinse the turkey thighs and dry. Sprinkle with spices. Heat the oil of your choice in a pan over medium heat. Add the turkey thighs to the pan and cook for 3 minutes on each side until browned.

Place the turkey thighs in a single layer over the onion mixture. Add the orange sections and cover. Cook for 4 hours in low heat.

Remove the turkey thighs from the slow cooker, then remove the bones and discard. Transfer to a plate.

To make a sauce, pour ¾ of the cooking liquid and orange sections into a pan.

Combine the flour of your choice and the remaining ¼ of the cooking liquid in a bowl. Whisk until smooth. Add flour mixture to the pan.

Bring the sauce to a boil and cook for 1 minute, stirring continuously until it thickens.

Pour sauce over turkey and serve.

Enjoy!

11. Poblano Pudding

Poblano pudding is a delicious Mexican theme buffet that is a good addition to any meal.

4 **poblano chilies** (chopped)
½ cup **coconut milk**
4 tbs **arrowroot flour** or **coconut flour**
2 tbs **coconut butter**
¼ tsp **salt**
3 cups **cauliflower rice**
1 tbs **coconut cream**
Cooking spray
2 **eggs**

Makes 8 servings
Calories: 175 per serving

Preheat the broiler and place the chilies on a baking sheet. Broil until darkened and charred, typically less than 10 minutes.

Place in a paper bag and close to seal. Set aside for 15 minutes.

Combine the coconut milk, the flour of your choice, coconut butter, salt and eggs in a slow cooker. Stir using a whisk until blended properly.

Add the cauliflower rice, coconut cream and chilies. Cover and cook on low heat for 2 ½ -3 hours.

Remove the lid and cook for another 15 minutes.

Enjoy!

12. Paleo Tortillas with Jicama Slaw

This dish has an exotic and spicy flavor, combining seasoning and spices. It contains the option to include some vinegar, which is a "gray ingredient" in the paleo diet and has been adopted by many that follow a paleo lifestyle. As always, choose organic meat.

2 lb. (900 g) **beef roast** (trimmed of fat)
½ **red onion** (diced)
1 inch fresh **ginger root**
2 tbs **sesame seeds**
10 **garlic cloves**
2 **jalapeños** (optional, diced)
2 tbs **balsamic vinegar** (optional)
6 **paleo tortillas** from recipe 9a

For the Slaw:
¼ cup **red onion** (diced)
½ **Jicama** (diced)
1 tsp **Asian dressing** (or other)
2 **limes**

Makes 6 servings
Calories: 210 per serving

Combine the red onion, ginger, sesame seeds, optional vinegar, jalapeños, garlic and beef in a slow cooker. Cover and cook for 9 hours in low heat.

Shred the beef using two forks.

Make the jicama slaw by combining the ingredients in the 2nd list. Stir to combine and serve on top of the tortillas.

Serve both and enjoy!

13. Garlic Chicken

This garlic chicken recipe is easy to prepare using common ingredients. As always, choose organic meat.

2 lb. (900 g) **boneless chicken breast** (cut into chunks)
¾ tsp **dried basil**
1/3 cup paleo **ketchup** (optionally self-made)
Pinch of **red pepper flakes**
3 **garlic cloves** (minced)
1/3 cup **paleo sauce** of your choice (optional)

Makes 8 servings
Calories: 180 per serving

Add the garlic, optional sauce, paleo ketchup and basil in a bowl. Add the chicken into the bottom of the pot and pour the mixture over.

Cook for 4 hours in low heat. Add water if the chicken seems to be drying.

Place the chicken in a baking sheet, then broil for 5 minutes to crisp the outside.

Enjoy!

14. Italian Tomato Meatballs

Most meatballs combine pork, beef and veal. This recipe uses a lighter sauce to intensify the flavor without adding much on calories and fat. As always, choose organic meat.

1 **egg**
1 tsp **salt**
1 **small onion** (minced)
6 **garlic cloves** (minced)
1 lb. (450 g) **lean ground beef**
½ tbs **olive oil** or **coconut oil**
14 oz. (400 g) **dice tomatoes**
2 tsp **Italian seasoning**
1 **bay leaf**
1 **egg white**
¼ **parsley** (minced)
2 lb. (900 g) **chicken** or **turkey sausage**
28 oz. (800g) **tomatoes** (crushed)
1 tsp **red pepper flakes**
1 cup **chicken broth**

Makes 8 servings
Calories: 210 per serving

Whisk the egg and egg white together in a bowl. Add the parsley, garlic cloves and ¼ of the onion.

Combine the beef and sausage and stir to mix.

Roll the mixture into balls. The mixture should be enough for 22-25 meatballs, depending on the size you make them. Add to a slow cooker.

Heat the oil of your choice in a pan over medium heat. Sauté the remaining ¾ of the onion for 5 minutes until fragrant and tender.

Add the red pepper flakes, Italian seasoning, and garlic. Stir for 30 seconds before adding the diced tomatoes, bay leaf, crushed tomatoes and chicken broth.

Pour the sauce over the meatballs in the slow cooker and cook for 6 hours in low heat.

Enjoy!

15. Thai Curry Beef

The combination of coconut milk and curry makes this dish interesting and delicious. It goes well with cauliflower rice or cabbage leaves. As always, choose organic meat.

1 lb. (450 g) **lean ground beef**
2 **garlic cloves** (minced)
1 tsp **red curry paste**
1 tsp **lime zest**
½ cup **coconut milk**
1 **medium leek** (sliced)
1 tsp **ginger** (minced)
1 ½ cup **tomato sauce**
2 tsp **lime juice**

Makes 4 servings
Calories: 220 per serving

Brown the ground beef in a pan, then add it to a slow cooker with garlic, red curry paste, lime, tomato sauce and leek. Cover and cook for 4 hours on high heat.

Stir in the lime juice and coconut milk. Cook for 15 more minutes before serving.

Enjoy!

16. Chicken and Cauliflower

This is a delicious Indian chicken dish filled with flavors. As always, choose organic meat.

1 lb. (450 g) **chicken breast** (cut into chunks)
1 tbs **coriander**
1 tsp **salt**
2 whole **jalapeños**
1 **onion** (diced)
1 tbs **pepper**
3 inch (7.6 cm) **ginger** (grated)
1 tbs **arrowroot flour** or **coconut flour**
1 lb. (450 g) **chicken thighs**
1 tbs **cumin**
2 tbs **coconut butter**
6 **garlic cloves** (minced)
3 tbs **garam masala**
4 cups **tomatoes** (crushed)
1 lb. (450 g) **cauliflower florets**
1 cup nonfat **coconut milk**

Makes 10 servings
Calories: 200 per serving

Season the chicken with the cumin, salt, and coriander. Place at the bottom of a slow cooker. Add the jalapeños on top of the chicken.

Melt the coconut butter in a pan over medium heat. Add garlic and onion. Fry for 6 minutes or until fragrant and brown. Add the garam masala and ginger. Stir to combine.

Add the tomatoes to the slow cooker and pour the sauce over the chicken. Set heat to low and cook for 6 hours until the chicken is tender.

Add the cauliflower 1 hour before the chicken is done. Stir in the flour of your choice and coconut milk.

Cover for 10 minutes until the sauce is thick.

Enjoy!

17. Beef and Tomatoes

This is a delicious meal that can be paired with paleo noodles, the paleo zucchini noodles from section 1, or cauliflower rice from section 1. The tomato sauce and beef blends very well to create a delicious sauce. As always, choose organic meat.

2.5 lb. (1.1 kg) **lean beef chuck**
½ **onion** (diced)
4 **garlic cloves** (minced)
15 oz. (425 g) **tomatoes** (crushed)
15 oz. (425 g) **tomatoes** (diced)
2 tbs **thyme** (chopped)
2 tbs **rosemary** (minced)
1 **celery** (diced)
1 **carrot** (peeled, diced)
2 **bay leaves**

Makes 10 servings
Calories: 170 per serving

Combine the celery, onion, garlic and carrots in a slow cooker and season with salt and pepper.

Add the remaining ingredients and stir to mix.

Cover, set heat to low and cook for 6 hours or until the meat is tender.

Enjoy!

18. Coconut Chicken

This recipe is rich in ingredients, taste and health benefits. As always, choose organic meat.

2 lb. (900 g) **chicken breast** (cubed)
1 **shallot** (finely chopped)
2 tbs **coconut butter**
4 **garlic cloves** (minced)
2 tsp **garam masala**
1 tsp **cumin** (ground)
¾ cup **coconut milk**
2 ¼ tsp **cayenne peppers**
1 pinch **black pepper**
1 tbs **coconut oil**
¼ **white onion** (chopped)
2 tsp **lemon juice**
1 inch (2.5 cm) **ginger** (minced)
1 tsp **chili powder**
1 **bay leaf**
1 cup **tomato sauce**
1 pinch **salt**

Makes 6 servings
Calories: 240 per serving

Combine the shallots, onion, garlic, garam masala, chili powder, cumin, cayenne, bay leaf, lemon juice, tomato sauce and ginger in a blender and blend until smooth.

Combine the chicken breast, salt, paper, coconut oil, coconut butter and blended mix in a slow cooker. Cover, set heat to low and cook for 4 hours.

Taste and adjust the seasoning as needed.

19. Apple Rosemary Pork

This is a very satisfying dish that combines the taste of apples and pork. It ranks among my personal favorite meals. Choose coconut oil over olive oil for the most health benefits and remember to use organic meat.

3 lbs. (1.36 kg) **pork roast**
2 **apples** (peeled, cored, chopped)
1 tbs fresh **rosemary**
2 tbs **olive oil** or **coconut oil**
1 **onion** (chopped)
2 cloves **garlic** (crushed)
2 cups of **apple cider**
1 tsp minced fresh **thyme**
Salt and ground **pepper**

Makes 6 servings
Calories: 220 per serving

Heat the oil of your choice in a pan over medium heat. Add the pork and cook for 10 minutes until browned.

Transfer to a slow cooker, saving some of the oil. Place the onion in the pan, then cook for 5 minutes in the saved oil. Add the apples and garlic to the pan and cook for 5 more minutes. Transfer to the slow cooker.

Add the rest of the ingredients in the slow cooker. Cover, set heat to low and cook for 7 hours.

Taste and season with salt and pepper as needed.

Enjoy!

20. Chicken Family Dinner

This slow cooker chicken recipe is perfect for a family dinner or get-together. It is tender and full of flavor. Remember to use organic meat.

3 lb. (1.36 kg) **skinless chicken thighs**
2 **celery stalks** (chopped)
12 oz. (340 g) **tomatoes** (diced)
1 **red** or **green pepper** (chopped)
2 tsp **oregano**
2 tsp **salt**
1 tsp **red pepper flakes**
1 large **white onion** (sliced)
6 oz. (170 g) **tomato paste**
1 lb. (450 g) **mushrooms** (sliced)
6 **garlic cloves** (minced)
1 ½ tsp **basil** (dried)

Makes 11 servings
Calories: 215 per serving

Combine all of the ingredients in a bowl except for the chicken, onion and celery.

Layer the celery and onions in a slow cooker.

Season the chicken thighs with salt and pepper. Place on top of the celery and onions.

Pour the mixture in the bowl on top. Cover, set heat to low and cook for 8 hours.

This dish tends to taste better the next day.

Enjoy!

Section 3: Soups and Stews

1. French Sausage Cassoulet

A cassoulet is a slow cooked casserole from the south of France. This one contains bacon and sausage flavors that are perfect for meat lovers. You can let the soup cook for a longer time, if your wish to have a thicker consistency. Remember to use organic meat.

2 **bacon slices**
1 tsp **dried thyme**
3 **garlic cloves** (minced)
½ tsp **black pepper** (ground)
15 oz. (425 g) **mushrooms** (chopped)
15 oz. (425 g) **cauliflower rice**
8 oz. **sausage**
8 tsp **fresh leaf parsley** (chopped)
2 cups **onion** (chopped)
½ tsp **rosemary** (dried)
½ tsp **salt**
30 oz. (850 g) **tomatoes** (diced)
16 oz. **lean boneless pork loin** (cubed)

Makes 8 servings
Calories: 220 per serving

Cook the bacon in a skillet over medium heat until brown and crispy. Remove the bacon and crumble, then set aside to cool.

Add the thyme, garlic, rosemary and onion in a pan. Cook until tender and fragrant for about 3 minutes.

Add the crumbled bacon, pepper, salt and tomatoes and bring to a boil. Remove from heat.

Add the mushrooms, cauliflower rice, sausage and pork. Stir to combine. Place the mixture in the slow cooker and top with the tomatoes.

Repeat the layers and cook for 5 hours in low heat. Ladle into soup bowls. Sprinkle with parsley.

Enjoy!

2. Bacon Coconut Soup

Potato soup is a classic and needs no introduction. As always, remember to use organic meat.

3 **bacon slices**
3 lbs. (1.36 kg) **sweet potatoes** (peeled, sliced)
½ cup **water**
½ tsp **salt**
2 cups **coconut milk**
½ cup **coconut cream**
1 cup **onion** (chopped)
30 oz. (850 g) **chicken broth**
½ tsp **black pepper** (ground)
4 tsp **fresh chives** (chopped)

Makes 8 servings
Calories: 235 per serving

Cook the bacon in a large pan until crispy. Transfer to a plate and reserve about 2 tbs of liquid in the pan. Crumble the bacon. Add onions to the pan and sauté for 3 minutes.

Combine the onion, potato slices, chicken broth, salt, pepper and ½ cup of water in a slow cooker. Cover and cook for 8 hours on low heat until the potatoes are tender.

Mash the soup and add the coconut milk.

Set the heat to high and cook for another 20 minutes.

Ladle into soup bowls. Top with coconut cream. Sprinkle with chives and bacon.

Enjoy!

3. Paleo Pozole

Pozole (aka posole) is a well-known Mexican soup or stew. The spicy flavor from the chilies make this dish perfect for cold weather. This version of Pazole eliminates the chicken and corn that is normally added to it. Instead, we use cauliflower rice, which is no grain and suitable for the paleo diet.

8 cups **vegetable broth**
2 **jalapeños** (seeded)
Salt and **pepper** to taste
4 **garlic cloves**
1 tbs dried **oregano**
3 **zucchini** (chopped)
2 **poblano peppers**
1 lb. (450 g) **tomatillos**
1 small bunch **cilantro**
60 oz. (1.7 kg) **cauliflower rice**
For garnish:
Shredded **cabbage**, **radishes**, **lime**, **jalapeños** or **avocado**

Makes 8 servings
Calories: 210 per serving

Combine the cilantro, cauliflower rice, tomatillos, peppers, oregano, salt, pepper, garlic and cilantro in a blender.

Pour the vegetable broth and blend until smooth. Taste and adjust the seasoning as necessary.

Pour the mixture in a slow cooker and cook for 4 hours on high heat. Add the zucchini and continue to cook for 30 minutes.

Ladle into soup bowls and use the garnish of your choice.

This dish can be served with baked sweet potatoes, cabbage and lime juice.

4. Cauliflower Soup

This healthy soup is packed with vegetables and rich in taste.

1 **cauliflower head** (cut into florets)
1 **onion** (diced)
2 **garlic cloves** (diced)
¼ cup **arrowroot flour** or **coconut flour**
1 cup **coconut milk**
1 cup **carrots** (diced)
3 **celery stalks**
4 cups **vegetable broth**
Salt and **pepper**

Makes 8 servings
Calories: 200 calories per serving

Combine the carrots, celery, cauliflower, garlic and broth in a slow cooker. Cook for 4 hours in low heat until the vegetables are tender.

Stir in the coconut milk. Add the flour of your choice and increase to medium heat. Cook for 1 more hour until the soup thickens.

Season the soup with salt and pepper. Use the blender to process the soup.

Enjoy

5. Sweet Potato Sausage Stew

This lentil stew has a spicy taste, combining a jalapeño with sweet potatoes and spinach. It goes very well with eggs.

1/3 lb. (150 g) **chicken sausage**
1 **celery** (chopped)
1 **sweet potato** (chopped)
3 cups **spinach**
½ tsp **cumin**
2 tbs **tomato paste**
¼ tsp **salt**
4 cups **chicken broth**
½ **onion** (diced)
1 **carrot** (chopped)
1 cup dry **lentils**
1 **jalapeño**
1 **garlic cloves** (minced)
1 **thyme sprigs**
¼ tsp **pepper**

Makes 5 servings
Calories: 150 calories per serving

Fry the chicken sausage until brown, then drain the fat. Place in a slow cooker.

Add the remaining ingredients to the cooker and cook for 5 hours on low heat.

Taste and season with salt and pepper.

You can store this dish in an airtight container and freeze it for about a week.

Enjoy

6. Traditional Mexican Beef Stew

This recipe combines traditional beef stew with spices like chili powder and chipotle peppers. As always, choose organic meat from free range animals. This recipe contains cocoa, an ingredient in dark bitter chocolate that is healthy and contains a lot of antioxidants. It is fine for the paleo diet.

1/3 cup **arrowroot flour** or **coconut flour**
1 tbs **ancho chili pepper** (ground)
1 tbs **coconut butter**
¼ tsp **black pepper** (ground)
1 red **bell pepper** (chopped)
14 oz. (400) **tomatoes** (diced)
1 tbs **unsweetened cocoa**
2 **beef briskets** (trimmed fat)
½ tsp **salt**
1 **green bell pepper** (chopped)
1 **yellow onion** (chopped)
1 ½ cups **beef broth**
1 tbs **adobo sauce**

Makes 7 servings
Calories: 200 per serving

Combine the ancho chili, salt, pepper, flour and cocoa in a small bowl. Coat the beef brisket in the flour of your choice and set aside.

Heat the coconut butter in a slow cooker and brown the brisket on each side. Transfer to plate and set aside.

Add the onion and pepper to the cooker. Cook for 5 minutes until the onions are fragrant and tender.

Add the beef broth, chipotle sauce, pepper, flour and tomatoes. Stir to combine.

Bring to a simmer and return the brisket to the slow cooker. Cook for 3 hours on high heat until the meat is tender.

Use forks to shred the meat into pieces.

Adjust the seasoning as needed and add chipotle sauce.

Enjoy!

7. Brazilian Chicken Stew

This Brazilian dish is perfect for cold weather. It can be served as is or on top of cauliflower rice.

1 ½ cups **low salt chicken broth**
1 lb. (450 g) **skinless chicken breast**
6 **garlic cloves**
½ cup **water**
7 oz. (225 g) **onion** (chopped)
1 **green** bell **pepper** (chopped)
6 **skinless boneless chicken thighs**
4 cups **cilantro leaves** (chopped)
2 large **jalapeños** (seeded)
1 **red bell pepper** (chopped)
1 lb. (450 g) **sweet potatoes** (peeled, chopped)
1 tsp **cumin** (ground)
Salt and **pepper** (ground)

Makes 7 servings
Calories: 220 per serving

Combine the water, cilantro, garlic, onion, salt, pepper, red pepper, green pepper, cumin and jalapeños in a blender, then blend until smooth.

Pour the mixture into a slow cooker and add the chicken. Cook for 2 hours on high heat until the meat is cooked through.

Add the broth until the sauce thickens. Taste and adjust the seasoning with salt and pepper as needed.

Add the potatoes to the slow cooker and make sure that everything is submerged in the sauce. Cover and cook for 45 minutes on high heat until the potatoes are cooked through.

8. Vegetarian Spinach Stew

This stew is rich in vegetables, protein, and fiber. It is also a great vegetarian meal, but if you want to have a meat friendly dish, you can serve it with chicken as well.

4 **garlic cloves** (chopped)
1 ½ cups **tomato sauce**
1 tbs **coriander** (ground)
1 tsp **salt**
1 ½ cups (350 ml) **coconut milk**
2 tbs **ginger** (minced)
1 tbs **garam masala**
1 tbs **cumin** (ground)
1/8 tsp **cayenne pepper**
30 oz. (850 g) **thawed spinach**

Makes 8 servings
Calories: 201 per serving

Add all ingredients except for the spinach in a slow cooker. Cover and cook for 3 hours on high heat.

Wash and drain the spinach. Add to the cooker and cook for 1 more hour.

This dish goes well with cauliflower rice or baked sweet potatoes.

Enjoy!

9. Beefy Stew

This is a healthier version of the traditional stew. Cooking a stew in a slow cooker is easy and you can use any combination of vegetables for this dish. As always, choose organic meat to make it healthy.

1 ½ lb. (680 g) **lean beef** (cut into chunks)
½ lb. (225 g) **parsnips** (chopped)
3 **celery ribs** (chopped)
2 tbs **Worcestershire sauce**
2 cups **water**
2 **bay leaves**
1 tsp **paprika**
2 tbs **arrowroot flour** or **coconut flour**
1 tsp **salt**
½ tsp **pepper**
¼ tsp **allspice** (ground)
2 cups fat free **beef broth**

Makes 8 servings
Calories: 232 per serving

Heat the oil in a slow cooker over medium heat. Add the beef and brown on all sides.

Add water, garlic, bay leaves, smoked paprika, Worcestershire sauce and onion. Let it simmer for 90 minutes.

Add the parsnips, celery, potato, carrots, and broth. Cook for 1 hour or until the meat is tender and can be shredded easily. The total cooking time will largely depend on the size of the beef you are using.

Mix the flour of your choice with water and stir to combine. Pour into the stew and bring to a boil.

Remove from heat and set aside before serving. This stew tastes best after storing it for two days, so consider preparing it in advance.

Enjoy!

10. Chicken Paleo-Noodle Soup

Chicken noodle soup is a classic favorite in many families. However, we need to substitute regular pasta with the paleo noodles or paleo zucchini noodles from section 1. Remember to use organic meat.

1 tbs **olive oil** or **coconut oil**
1 ½ lbs. **skinless, boneless chicken breast** or **thighs**
2 **cups onion** (chopped)
1 tbs **rosemary**
8 oz. (225 g) **mushrooms** (pre-sliced)
6 oz. (170 g) package **baby spinach**
½ tsp fresh **black pepper** (ground)
1 ½ lbs. (680 g) **skinless chicken thighs**
1 tsp **salt**
6 cups **chicken broth**
1 cup **celery** (chopped)
10 oz. (280 g) **carrot** (shredded)
1/3 cup **parsley** (chopped)
¼ cup **lemon juice**
4 cups **paleo noodles** or **Zucchini noodles**

Makes 11 servings
Calories: 250 per serving

Combine the oil, ½ tsp of salt and paleo noodles of your choice in a large bowl, then toss to coat.

Mix the chicken broth, chicken breast, onion, celery, rosemary, carrots, mushrooms, parsley, spinach and the remaining ½ tsp of salt in a slow cooker. Bring to a boil and simmer for 25-30 minutes.

Remove the chicken, set aside and allow to cool. Shred using a fork.

Add the carrots and mushroom to the cooker. Reduce the heat and cook until the carrots are tender.

Add the parsley, shredded chicken and spinach. Cook until the spinach wilts.

Add the paleo noodles, lemon juice and pepper. Cook for 10 more minute.

Enjoy!

Section 4: Appetizers and Side Dishes

1. Bacon with Collard Greens

This dish can be a great appetizer or side dish to pork or mashed sweet potatoes. This recipe contains the option to include some vinegar, which is a "gray ingredient" in the paleo diet and has been adopted by many that follow a paleo lifestyle.

3 **bacon slices**
16 oz. (450) **collard greens** (chopped)
2 **garlic cloves** (minced)
1 ½ cups (350 ml) **chicken broth**
1 cup **onion** (chopped)
¼ tsp **salt**
1 **bay leaf**
3 tbs **balsamic vinegar** (optional)

Makes 5 servings
Calories: 80 per serving

Cook the bacon in a frying pan until crispy. Transfer to a plate and crumble.

Add onions and sauté for 5 minutes until fragrant and soft.

Add the collard greens and cook until the vegetables are starting to wilt. Stir occasionally.

Remove the collard greens and put them in a bowl, then combine the salt, garlic cloves, bay leaf and chicken broth in a slow cooker. Cover and cook for 4 hours in low heat.

Add the optional vinegar to the greens before serving with bacon.

2. Paleo Bolognese

This classic Italian dish needs no introduction. However, to conform to the paleo diet, we need to serve it with paleo noodles or paleo zucchini noodles from section 1 instead of pasta. Remember to use organic meat.

1 ¾ **cups onion** (chopped)
½ cup **carrots** (chopped)
8 oz. (225 g) **beef** (ground)
8 oz. (225 g) **veal** (ground)
¼ cup **parsley** (chopped)
1 tsp **black pepper** (ground)
¼ tsp **cinnamon** (ground)
1 **bay leaf**
2/3 cup **celery** (chopped)
6 **garlic cloves** (minced)
8 oz. (225 g) **lean pork** (ground)
1 ½ cups **tomatoes** (crushed)
1 cup **beef broth**
2 tbs **tomato paste**
1 tsp **thyme** (dried)
½ tsp **oregano** (dried)
¼ tsp **salt**

Makes 6 servings
Calories: 235 per serving

Add the carrot, celery, onion and garlic in a pan, then sauté for 4 minutes over medium heat.

Add the veal, beef and pork. Coat with the vegetable mixture. Sauté for a few more minutes until the meat is browned. Stir the mixture to crumble.

Remove the meat and place in a slow cooker.

Add the tomatoes and the remaining ingredients. Cook for 8 hours in low heat, then remove the bay leaf. Before it is done, prepare the paleo noodles of your choice.

This dish can be stored in the freezer for a week.

Enjoy!

3. Sweet Potato Vegetable Dish

This is a delicious side dish that can be topped with crumbled bacon. This recipe contains the option to include some vinegar, which is a "gray ingredient" in the paleo diet and has been adopted by many that follow a paleo lifestyle. Remember to use organic meat.

1 ½ lb. (680 g) **sweet potatoes**
1 lb. **carrots**
¾ cup **cranberries** (dried)
3 tbs **olive oil** or **coconut oil**
1 tsp **salt**
1/3 cup **flat leaf parsley** (chopped)
1 lb. (450 g) **parsnips**
2 large **red onions** (chopped)
2 tbs **balsamic vinegar** (optional)
½ tsp **pepper** (ground)

Makes 6 servings
Calories: 180 per serving

Combine the onions, carrots, parsnips and cranberries in a slow cooker. Make sure to layer the sweet potatoes on top.

Whisk the oil of your choice, optional balsamic vinegar, salt and ground pepper in a bowl and pour on top of the vegetables.

Cover and cook for 4 hours in low heat until the vegetables are tender.

Sprinkle with the parsley before serving.

Enjoy!

4. Pepper Mushrooms in Bouillon

This spicy recipe is rich in taste and easy to prepare. It works very well as a side dish for sweet potatoes.

½ lb. (225 g) **mushrooms**
1 **red bell pepper** (chopped)
3 oz. (85 g) **pepperoni slices**
1 **chicken bouillon cube**
¼ tsp **red pepper** (ground)
1 ½ cups **cauliflower rice**
4 **green onions** (chopped)
1 **jalapeño pepper** (diced)
2 cups **hot water**
½ tsp **salt**
15 oz. (425 g) **Mexican stewed tomatoes**

Makes 12 servings
Calories: 200 per serving

Combine all of the ingredients except for the tomatoes and cauliflower rice in a slow cooker. Cover and cook for 8 hours in low heat.

Add the cauliflower rice and tomatoes. Cover and cook for another 30 minutes.

Enjoy!

5. Sausage and Apple Stuffing

This stuffing is perfect for thanksgiving. We have been using it in our family for several years. Remember to use organic meat for maximum health benefits. Instead of the cauliflower rice, you can also use paleo bread crumbs. There are many paleo breads to choose from.

8 oz. (425 g) **pork sausage**, (browned, drained)
5 cups **mushrooms**
3 cups **cauliflower rice**
1 1/2 tsp **sage** (rubbed)
1/2 tsp **black pepper**
1/2 cup **chicken broth**
1 1/2 cups **celery** (diced)
3 tbs **coconut butter** (melted)
1 1/2 cups **onion** (chopped)
1 1/2 cups **apples** (chopped)
1 tsp **salt**

Makes 8 servings
Calories: 267 per serving

Heat the coconut butter in a slow cooker on low heat. Add the sausage to the cooker and brown it.

Add the vegetables, apples, cauliflower rice, mushrooms, seasonings, and ½ cup chicken broth. Stir to coat.

Cover, set heat on high and cook for 2 ½ to 3 hours.

If you need more moisture, you can add an extra ¼ cup of broth before serving. Stir to mix.

Enjoy!

6. Zucchini Dish

This dish combines many flavors, ranging from the exotic quality of coconuts to the tanginess of herbs.

2 zucchinis
5 cups (1.2 liters) **chicken broth**
½ cup **shallots** (chopped)
1 tsp **oregano** (crushed, dried)
3 tbs **coconut butter**
1 tbs **olive oil** or **coconut oil**
1 **yellow sweet pepper** (chopped)
2 cups **cauliflower rice**
3 **garlic cloves** (minced)
3 cups **mushrooms** (sliced)
Italian flat leaf parsley

Makes 12 servings
Calories: 205 per serving

Lightly coat the slow cooker with oil or cooking spray.

Add the zucchini, cauliflower rice, oregano, salt and pepper, chicken broth, garlic, and shallots. Cover and cook for 4 hours in high heat.

Add the coconut butter, then remove from heat. Set aside for 15 minutes. Pour the vegetable broth, if the dish is too dry.

Heat the oil of your choice in a pan. Cook the sliced mushrooms, then transfer to plate.

Top with sweet pepper and parsley.

Enjoy!

7. Sweet Potatoes and Bacon

This side dish is a different treat from the usual sweet potatoes. Instead, use herbs to add more flavor to the dish. As always, use organic meat.

4 lb. (1.8 kg) **sweet potatoes** (peeled, sliced)
2 tbs **coconut oil** (optional)
½ tsp **dried leaf sage** (crushed)
2 tbs **coconut butter**
½ cup **orange concentrate**
1 ½ tsp **salt**
½ tsp **dried thyme**
4 **crispy bacon slices**

Makes 9 servings
Calories: 180 per serving

Place the sweet potatoes in a slow cooker.

Mix the orange concentrate, optional coconut oil, sage, thyme and salt in a bowl.

Pour the mixture over the sweet potatoes and toss to coat. Add the coconut butter.

Cook in low heat for 6 hours.

Sprinkle with crumbled bacon before serving.

Enjoy!

8. Sweet Potato Ginger Dish

This side dish is a personal favorite. It combines health and sweetness, containing no sugars and few calories. Specifically, this dish is great in winter and around Christmas time.

2 **Granny Smith apples** (peeled, chopped)
1 ½ lb. (680 g) **sweet potatoes** (peeled, cut)
2 tbs **cranberries** (dried)
1/2 cup **water**
1/8 tsp **black pepper** (ground)
1 1/2 tsp **fresh ginger** (grated)
1/2 tsp **salt**
1/4 tsp **nutmeg** (ground)
1/4 cup **coconut oil** (melted)
1/2 tsp **cinnamon** (ground)

Makes 8 servings
Calories: 103 per serving

Combine the sweet potatoes, cranberries, apples, cinnamon, ginger, salt, nutmeg and pepper in a slow cooker. Stir to combine. Add water and coconut oil.

Cover and cook on low heat for 5 ½ hours, or 2 ½ hours on high heat.

Enjoy!

9. Barley Squash Spinach

This dish is easy to make and very nutritious without loading up on calories. Squash in particular provides many important vitamins.

2 lb. (910 h) **butternut squash** (peeled, cubed)
1 **medium onion** (cut into wedges)
1 ¾ cups (410 ml) **vegetables broth**
3 **garlic cloves** (minced)
¼ tsp **black pepper** (ground)
10 oz. (280 g) **spinach** (chopped)
1 cup **barley**
½ cup **water**
¾ tsp **salt**

Makes 6 servings
Calories: 162 per serving

Place the squash, spinach, broth, water, onion, barley, garlic, salt and pepper in a slow cooker.

Cover and cook for 7 hours in low heat, or 3 hours in high heat.

Remove and let it sit for 10 minutes before serving.

Enjoy!

10. Broccoli and Cauliflower in Sauce

This recipe provides a wonderful blend of Alfredo sauce and coconut oil. The herbs add a delicious flavor to the dish.

4 cups **broccoli florets**
14 oz. (400 ml) **Alfredo sauce**
1 **large onion** (chopped)
¼ tsp **black pepper** (ground)
4 cups **cauliflower florets**
10 tbs **coconut oil**
1 tsp **thyme** (dried)
½ cup **almonds** (sliced)

Makes 10 servings
Calories: 170 calories per serving

Place the cauliflower, broccoli, coconut oil, onion, pasta sauce, thyme and pepper in a small slow cooker.

Cook for 7 hours in low heat or 3 hours in high heat.

Stir occasionally. Adjust the seasoning as desired and sprinkle with almonds.

Enjoy!

11. Sweet Potatoes in Broth

Mashed potatoes are easy to make and is one of the classic side dishes that can be served with any meal.

3 lb. (1.36 kg) **sweet potatoes** (peeled)
1 **bay leaf**
1 cup **coconut milk**
1 tsp **salt**
6 **garlic cloves** (halved)
3 ¼ cups (770 ml) **chicken broth**
¼ cup **coconut butter**
Fresh **black pepper** (ground)

Makes 11 servings
Calories: 130 per serving

Place the sweet potatoes, garlic and bay leaf in a slow cooker. Add the broth.

Cover, set heat to low and cook for 4 hours.

Drain the potatoes in a colander. Catch the cooking liquid in a bowl below, then remove the bay leaf and discard it.

Return the potatoes to the slow cooker. Mash using a fork or a masher.

Combine the coconut milk and coconut butter in a saucepan. Heat until the butter melts. Add the coconut milk mixture to the slow cooker and return some of the cooking liquid until desired consistency is reached.

Transfer to a bowl, sprinkle with ground pepper and garnish with bay leaves.

Enjoy!

12. Cabbage with Apples

This is a wonderful and simple side dish that adds an apple taste to any meal. It works very well with chicken.

1 medium-sized **cabbage** (chopped)
2 **tart apples** (diced)
1 tbs **olive oil** or **coconut oil**
3 tbs **spicy mustard**
1 cup **apple juice**
1 **onion** (quartered, sliced)
1/2 cup **chicken broth**
½ tsp **salt**
1/8 tsp **pepper** (ground)

Makes 7 servings
Calories: 87 per serving

Heat the oil of your choice in a slow cooker over low heat. Add the cabbage, apples, onion, and season with salt and pepper. Stir to mix.

Combine the chicken broth, mustard, and apple juice in a bowl. Whisk to combine. Add the mixture to the cooker.

Cover and cook for 7 hours in low heat. Stir every 2 hours.

With a slotted spoon, remove from the cooker to a bowl or plates.

Enjoy!

13. Carrot Garlic Soup

This carrot garlic soup provides a delicious and healthy meal for the whole family. Remember to use organic meat.

2 lb. (910 g) **carrots**
3 **garlic cloves** (finely chopped)
1 tsp **curry powder**
½ cup **coconut cream**
8 oz. (225 g) **shrimps** (peeled, cooked)
6 **white and green scallions**
2 tbs **fresh ginger** (chopped)
2 ½ cups low sodium **chicken broth**
1 pinch **salt**
Cilantro to sprinkle (optional)

Makes 6 servings
Calories: 177 per serving

Combine the scallions, ginger, curry powder, garlic and carrots in a slow cooker.

Add 2 cups of water, then bring to a boil. Cook for 7 to 8 hours in low heat until carrots are tender.

Remove from heat and allow to cool slightly.

Puree the soup in batches, then return to the slow cooker.

Add the coconut cream and season with salt until completely heated through.

Ladle the soup into bowls and top with optional cilantro.

Enjoy!

14. Acorn Squash Stew

This is a slow cooker soup made from chicken broth and squash. As always, use organic meat and coconut options for maximum health benefits.

3 cups **cauliflower rice**
2 **chicken breasts** (diced)
1 cube **vegetable bouillon**
2 tbs **pesto**
1 **onion** (diced)
4 tbs **coconut cream**
1 **thyme** (chopped)
1 **acorn squash**
1 ½ cups (350 ml) **chicken broth**
1 tbs **garlic** (minced)
4 cups **water**
1 fresh **sage**
1 **basil** (chopped)

Makes 6 servings
Calories: 138 per serving

Cut the squash in half then bake at high heat. Bake until tender.

Prepare the cauliflower rice. Set aside.

Place all of the ingredients in a slow cooker except for the coconut cream.

Cook for about 12 hours. Add water, if the mixture starts to dry out.

Add the coconut cream and season it with salt before serving.

Enjoy!

15. Coconut Mushrooms and Cauliflower

This is a delicious coconut recipe, healthy and very easy to prepare.

1 cup **mushrooms**
1 **onion** (large, finely diced)
14 oz. (400 ml) **coconut milk**
2 **cloves garlic** (minced)
1 tsp **red pepper flakes**
3 cups **chicken broth**
1 ½ cups **cauliflower rice**
½ tsp **salt**

Makes 8 servings
Calories: 228 per serving

Combine the mushrooms, red pepper flakes, onion, garlic, coconut milk and chicken broth in a slow cooker.

Stir in cauliflower rice and salt. Cover and cook on low heat for 9hours until everything is tender.

Enjoy!

Appendix: References

If you are not in the sciences, let me quickly explain what this section is about. In all proper research, it is obligatory that you cite the scientific sources of information that your research paper, article or books used or touched on. As a good scientist, when I studied the Paleolithic diet, I assembled a list of all the papers I went through. Below, you find this list.

Almost all scientific journals out there are pay-only and quite expensive. If you are at a university, you should have free access to most of these papers from the computers on your campus. This is because universities pay for membership in most journals, so any of their researchers and students can use them.

Lindeberg, Staffan (June 2005). "Palaeolithic diet ('stone age' diet)". *Scandinavian Journal of Food & Nutrition* **49** (2): 75–7. doi:10.1080/11026480510032043.

Lindeberg, Staffan; Cordain, Loren; Eaton, S. Boyd (September 2003). "Biological and Clinical Potential of a Palaeolithic Diet". *Journal of Nutritional and Environmental Medicine* **13** (3): 149–60. doi:10.1080/13590840310001619397.

Kligler, Benjamin & Lee, Roberta A. (eds.) (2004). "Paleolithic diet". *Integrative medicine*. McGraw-Hill Professional. pp. 139–40. ISBN 0-07-140239-X.

Eaton, S.Boyd; Cordain, Loren; Lindeberg, Staffan (2002). "Evolutionary Health Promotion: A Consideration of Common Counterarguments". *Preventive Medicine* **34** (2): 119–23. doi:10.1006/pmed.2001.0966. PMID 11817904.

Lindeberg S, Jönsson T, Granfeldt Y, Borgstrand E, Soffman J, Sjöström K, Ahrén B (September 2007). "A Palaeolithic diet improves glucose tolerance more than a Mediterranean-like diet in individuals with ischaemic heart disease". *Diabetologia* **50** (9): 1795–807. doi:10.1007/s00125-007-0716-y. PMID 17583796.

Frassetto, L A; Schloetter, M; Mietus-Synder, M; Morris, R C; Sebastian, A (2009). "Metabolic and physiologic improvements from consuming a paleolithic, hunter-gatherer type diet". *European Journal of Clinical Nutrition* **63** (8): 947–955. doi:10.1038/ejcn.2009.4. PMID 19209185.

Cannon, Geoffrey (June 2006). "Out of the Box". *Public Health Nutrition* **9** (4): 411–14. doi:10.1079/PHN2006959.

Nestle, Marion (May 1999). "Animal v. plant foods in human diets and health: is the historical record unequivocal?". *Proceedings of the Nutrition Society* **58** (2): 211–18. doi:10.1017/S0029665199000300. PMID 10466159.

Richards, Michael P. (December 2002). "A brief review of the archaeological evidence for Palaeolithic and Neolithic subsistence". *European Journal of Clinical Nutrition* **56** (12): 1270–78. doi:10.1038/sj.ejcn.1601646. PMID 12494313.

Milton, Katharine (2002). "Hunter-gatherer diets: wild foods signal relief from diseases of affluence". In Ungar, Peter S. & Teaford, Mark F. *Human Diet: Its Origins and Evolution.* Westport, CT: Bergin and Garvey. pp. 111–22. ISBN 0897897366.

Naugler, Christopher T. (September 1, 2008). "Evolutionary medicine: Update on the relevance to family practice". *Canadian Family Physician* **54** (9): 1265–9. PMC 2553465. PMID 18791103.

Eaton, S.Boyd; Strassman, Beverly I; Nesse, Randolph M; Neel, James V; Ewald, Paul W; Williams, George C; Weder, Alan B; Eaton, Stanley B et al. (2002). "Evolutionary Health Promotion". *Preventive Medicine* **34** (2): 109–18. doi:10.1006/pmed.2001.0876. PMID 11817903.

Eaton, S. Boyd; Konner, Melvin (1985). "Paleolithic Nutrition — A Consideration of Its Nature and Current Implications". *The New England Journal of Medicine* **312** (5): 283–9. doi:10.1056/NEJM198501313120505. PMID 2981409.

Sirota, Lorraine Handler; Greenberg, George (1989). "Book reviews". *Biofeedback and Self-Regulation* **14** (4): 347–54. doi:10.1007/BF00999126.

Vines, Gail (August 26, 1989). "Palaeolithic recipe for the clean life / Review of 'The Stone-Age Health Programme' by S. Boyd Eaton, Marjorie Shostak and Melvin Konner". New Scientist. Retrieved January 19, 2008.

Lindeberg, S; & Lundh, B (March 1993). "Apparent absence of stroke and ischaemic heart disease in a traditional Melanesian island: a clinical study in Kitava". *Journal of Internal Medicine* **233** (3): 269–75. doi:10.1111/j.1365-2796.1993.tb00986.x. PMID 8450295.

O'Keefe, James H.; & Cordain, Loren (January 2004). "Cardiovascular disease resulting from a diet and lifestyle at odds with our Paleolithic genome: how to become a 21st-century hunter-gatherer" (PDF). *Mayo Clinic Proceedings* **79** (1): 101–08. doi:10.4065/79.1.101. PMID 14708953.

Cordain, Loren; Eaton, S Boyd; Sebastian, Anthony; Mann, Neil; Lindeberg, Staffan; Watkins, Bruce A; O'Keefe, James H; Brand-Miller, Janette (2005). "Origins and evolution of the Western diet: health implications for the 21st century". *American Journal of Clinical Nutrition* **81** (2): 341–54. PMID 15699220.

Cordain L, Watkins BA, Florant GL, Kelher M, Rogers L, Li Y (March 2002). "Fatty acid analysis of wild ruminant tissues: evolutionary implications for reducing diet-related chronic disease". *European Journal of Clinical Nutrition* **56** (3): 181–91. doi:10.1038/sj.ejcn.1601307. PMID 11960292.

Cordain L, Eaton SB, Sebastian A, Mann N, Lindeberg S, Watkins BA, O'Keefe JH, Brand-Miller J (1 August 2005). "Reply to SC Cunnane" (PDF). *The American Journal of Clinical Nutrition* **82** (2): 483–84. PMID 16087997.

Cordain L, Miller JB, Eaton SB, Mann N, Holt SH, Speth JD (1 March 2000). "Plant-animal subsistence ratios and macronutrient energy estimations in worldwide hunter-gatherer diets". *The American Journal of Clinical Nutrition* **71** (3): 682–92. PMID 10702160.

Cordain L, Eaton SB, Miller JB, Mann N, Hill K (March 2002). "The paradoxical nature of hunter-gatherer diets: meat based, yet non-atherogenic" (PDF). *European Journal of Clinical Nutrition* **56** (Suppl 1): S42–52. doi:10.1038/sj.ejcn.1601353. PMID 11965522.

Eaton SB, Eaton SB 3rd, Konner MJ (1997). "Paleolithic nutrition revisited: a twelve-year retrospective on its nature and implications" (PDF). *European Journal of Clinical Nutrition* **51** (4): 207–16. doi:10.1038/sj.ejcn.1600389. PMID 9104571.

Eaton, S. Boyd (2007). "The ancestral human diet: What was it and should it be a paradigm for contemporary nutrition?". *Proceedings of the Nutrition Society* **65** (1): 1–6. doi:10.1079/PNS2005471. PMID 16441938.

Frank W Booth et al. (2002). "Exercise and gene expression: physiological regulation of the human genome through physical activity". *J Physiol* **543** (Pt 2): 399–411. doi:10.1113/jphysiol.2002.019265. PMC 2290514. PMID 12205177.

Eaton, SB; Eaton, SB (2003). "An evolutionary perspective on human physical activity: Implications for health". *Comparative biochemistry and physiology. Part A, Molecular & integrative physiology* **136** (1): 153–9. doi:10.1016/S1095-6433(03)00208-3. PMID 14527637.

Ströhle, Alexander; Wolters, Maike; Hahn, Andreas (January 2007). "Carbohydrates and the diet–atherosclerosis connection—More between earth and heaven. Comment on the article 'The atherogenic potential of dietary carbohydrate'". *Preventive Medicine* **44** (1): 82–4. doi:10.1016/j.ypmed.2006.08.014. PMID 16997359.

Santos, J. L.; Saus, E.; Smalley, S. V.; Cataldo, L. R.; Alberti, G.; Parada, J.; Gratacòs, M.; Estivill, X. (2012). "Copy Number Polymorphism of the Salivary Amylase Gene: Implications in Human Nutrition Research". *Journal of Nutrigenetics and Nutrigenomics* **5** (3): 117–131. doi:10.1159/000339951. PMID 22965187.

Wilson, David S. (1994). "Adaptive genetic variation and human evolutionary psychology". *Ethology and Sociobiology* **15** (4): 219–35. doi:10.1016/0162-3095(94)90015-9.

Kopp, Wolfgang (January 2007). "Reply to the comment of Ströhle et al". *Preventive Medicine* **44** (1): 84–5. doi:10.1016/j.ypmed.2006.09.003.

Hawks J, Wang ET, Cochran GM, Harpending HC, Moyzis RK (December 2007). "Recent acceleration of human adaptive evolution". *Proc Natl Acad Sci U S A* **104** (52): 20753–8. doi:10.1073/pnas.0707650104. PMC 2410101. PMID 18087044.

Mahner, Martin; & Bunge, Mario (2001). "Function and functionalism: a synthetic perspective". *Philosophy of Science* **68** (1): 75–94. doi:10.1086/392867.

Milton, Katharine; & Demment, Montague W. (1 September 1988). "Digestion and passage kinetics of chimpanzees fed high and low fiber diets and comparison with human data" (PDF). *Journal of Nutrition* **118** (9): 1082–88. PMID 2843616.

Milton, Katharine (June 1999). "Nutritional characteristics of wild primate foods: do the diets of our closest living relatives have lessons for us?" (PDF). *Nutrition* **15** (6): 488–98. doi:10.1016/S0899-9007(99)00078-7. PMID 10378206.

Milton, Katharine (1999). "A hypothesis to explain the role of meat-eating in human evolution" (PDF). *Evolutionary Anthropology* **8** (1): 11–21. doi:10.1002/(SICI)1520-6505(1999)8:1<11::AID-EVAN6>3.0.CO;2-M.

Milton, Katharine (2000). "Back to basics: why foods of wild primates have relevance for modern human health" (PDF). *Nutrition* **16** (7–8): 481–83. doi:10.1016/S0899-9007(00)00293-8. PMID 10906529.

Piperno, D; Weiss, E., Hols, I., Nadel, D (2004). "Processing of wild cereal grains in the Upper Paleolithic revealed by starch grain analysis". *Nature* **430** (7000): 670–673. doi:10.1038/nature02734. PMID 15295598.

Revedin, Anna; Aranguren, B; Becattini, R; Longo, L; Marconi, E; Lippi, MM; Skakun, N; Sinitsyn, A et al. (2010). "Thirty thousand-year-old evidence of plant food processing". *Proc Natl Acad Sci U S A* **107** (44): 18815–9. doi:10.1073/pnas.1006993107. PMC 2973873. PMID 20956317.

Kris-Etherton, PM; Harris, WS; Appel, LJ; Nutrition, Committee (2003). "Fish Consumption, Fish Oil, Omega-3 Fatty Acids, and Cardiovascular Disease". *Arteriosclerosis, thrombosis, and vascular biology* **23** (2): e20–30.

Fairweather-Tait, Susan J. (October 29, 2003). "Human nutrition and food research: opportunities and challenges in the post-genomic era". *Phil. Trans. R. Soc. B* **358** (1438): 1709–27. doi:10.1098/rstb.2003.1377. PMC 1693270. PMID 14561328.

Jönsson T, Olsson S, Ahrén B, Bøg-Hansen TC, Dole A, Lindeberg S (2005). "Agrarian diet and diseases of affluence – Do evolutionary novel dietary lectins cause leptin resistance?". *BMC Endocrine Disorders* **5**: 10. doi:10.1186/1472-6823-5-10. PMC 1326203. PMID 16336696.

Leach, Jeff D. (2007). "Prebiotics in Ancient Diet". *Food Science and Technology Bulletin* **4** (1): 1–8. doi:10.1616/1476-2137.14801.

Collins, Christopher (January–March 2007). "Said Another Way: Stroke, Evolution, and the Rainforests: An Ancient Approach to Modern Health Care". *Nursing Forum* **42** (1): 39–44. doi:10.1111/j.1744-6198.2007.00064.x. PMID 17257394

Bellisari A. (March 2008). "Evolutionary origins of obesity". *Obesity Reviews* **9** (2): 165–180. doi:10.1111/j.1467-789X.2007.00392.x. PMID 18257754.

Strandvik, B. Eriksson, S. Garemo, M. Palsdottir, V. Samples, S. Pickova, J (March 4, 2008). "Is the relatively low intake of omega-3 fatty acids in Western diet contributing to the obesity epidemics?". *Lipid Technology* **20** (3): 57–59. doi:10.1002/lite.200800009.

Wood LE (October 2006). "Obesity, waist–hip ratio and hunter–gatherers". *BJOG: an International Journal of Obstetrics & Gynaecology* **113** (10): 1110–16. doi:10.1111/j.1471-0528.2006.01070.x. PMID 16972857.

O'Keefe JH Jr, Cordain L, Harris WH, Moe RM, Vogel R (June 2004). "Optimal low-density lipoprotein is 50 to 70 mg/dl: lower is better and physiologically normal". *Journal of the American College of Cardiology* (American College of Cardiology) **43** (11): 2142–46. doi:10.1016/j.jacc.2004.03.046. PMID 15172426.

O'Keefe JH Jr, Cordain L, Jones PG, Abuissa H. (July 2006). "Coronary artery disease prognosis and C-reactive protein levels improve in proportion to percent lowering of low-density lipoprotein". *The American Journal of Cardiology* **98** (1): 135–39. doi:10.1016/j.amjcard.2006.01.062. PMID 16784936.

Kopp, Wolfgang (May 2006). "The atherogenic potential of dietary carbohydrate". *Preventive Medicine* **42** (5): 336–42. doi:10.1016/j.ypmed.2006.02.003. PMID 16540158.

Tekol, Yalcin (April 2008). "Maternal and infantile dietary salt exposure may cause hypertension later in life". *Birth Defects Research Part B: Developmental and Reproductive Toxicology* **83** (2): 77–79. doi:10.1002/bdrb.20149. PMID 18330898.

Dedoussis GV, Kaliora AC, Panagiotakos DB (Spring 2007). "Genes, Diet and Type 2 Diabetes Mellitus: A Review". *Review of Diabetic Studies* **4** (1): 13–24. doi:10.1900/RDS.2007.4.13. PMC 1892523. PMID 17565412.

Sebastian A, Frassetto LA, Sellmeyer DE, Merriam RL, Morris RC Jr (1 December 2002). "Estimation of the net acid load of the diet of ancestral preagricultural Homo sapiens and their hominid ancestors". *The American Journal of Clinical Nutrition* **76** (6): 1308–16. PMID 12450898.

Morris RC Jr, Schmidlin O, Frassetto LA, Sebastian A (June 2006). "Relationship and interaction between sodium and potassium". *Journal of the American College of Nutrition* **25** (3): 262S–70S. PMID 16772638.

Lawlor, Debbie A; & Ness, Andy R (April 2003). "Commentary: The rough world of nutritional epidemiology: Does dietary fibre prevent large bowel cancer?". *International Journal of Epidemiology* **32** (2): 239–43. doi:10.1093/ije/dyg060. PMID 12714543.

Leach, Jeff D. (January 2007). "Evolutionary perspective on dietary intake of fibre and colorectal cancer". *European Journal of Clinical Nutrition* **61** (1): 140–42. doi:10.1038/sj.ejcn.1602486. PMID 16855539.

Cordain L, Eaton SB, Brand Miller J, Lindeberg S, Jensen C (April 2002). "An evolutionary analysis of the etiology and pathogenesis of juvenile-onset myopia". *Acta Ophthalmologica Scandinavica* **80** (2): 125–35. doi:10.1034/j.1600-0420.2002.800203.x. PMID 11952477.

Cordain L, Lindeberg S, Hurtado M, Hill K, Eaton SB, Brand-Miller J (December 2002). "Acne vulgaris: a disease of Western civilization". *Archives of Dermatology* **138** (12): 1584–90. doi:10.1001/archderm.138.12.1584. PMID 12472346

Keri, Jonette E; Nijhawan, Rajiv (August 2008). "Diet and acne". *Expert Review of Dermatology* **3** (4): 437–40. doi:10.1586/17469872.3.4.437.

Cunnane, Stephen C. (1 August 2005). "Origins and evolution of the Western diet: implications of iodine and seafood intakes for the human brain". *The American Journal of Clinical Nutrition* **82** (2): 483; author reply 483–4. PMID 16087997.

Solomons, Noel W (2008). "National food fortification: a dialogue with reference to Asia: balanced advocacy" (PDF). *Asia Pacific Journal of Clinical Nutrition* **17** (Suppl 1): 20–3. PMID 18296293.

Friis, Henrik (February 2007). "International nutrition and health". *Danish Medical Bulletin* **54** (1): 55–7. PMID 17349228.

Mann, Neil (September 2007). "Meat in the human diet: an anthropological perspective" (PDF). *Nutrition & Dietetics* **64** (4): S102–S107. doi:10.1111/j.1747-0080.2007.00194.x.

Cordain L, Miller JB, Eaton SB, Mann N (1 December 2000). "Macronutrient estimations in hunter-gatherer diets". *The American Journal of Clinical Nutrition* **72** (6): 1589–92. PMID 11101497.

Westman EC, Feinman RD, Mavropoulos JC, Vernon MC, Volek JS, Wortman JA, Yancy WS, Phinney SD (1 August 2007). "Low-carbohydrate nutrition and metabolism". *The American Journal of Clinical Nutrition* **86** (2): 276–84. PMID 17684196.

Colagiuri, Stephen; & Brand-Miller, Jennie (March 2002). "The 'carnivore connection'—evolutionary aspects of insulin resistance" (PDF). *European Journal of Clinical Nutrition* **56** (1): S30–5. doi:10.1038/sj.ejcn.1601351. PMID 11965520.

Plaskett, L. G. (September 2003). "On the Essentiality of Dietary Carbohydrate". *Journal of Nutritional & Environmental Medicine* **13** (3): 161–168. doi:10.1080/13590840310001619405.

Pérez-Guisado, J (2008). "Ketogenic diets: Additional benefits to the weight loss and unfounded secondary effects". *Archivos latinoamericanos de nutricion* **58** (4): 323–9. PMID 19368291

Westman, EC; Yancy Jr, WS; Mavropoulos, JC; Marquart, M; McDuffie, JR (2008). "The effect of a low-carbohydrate, ketogenic diet versus a low-glycemic index diet on glycemic control in type 2 diabetes mellitus". *Nutrition & metabolism* **5**: 36. doi:10.1186/1743-7075-5-36. PMC 2633336. PMID 19099589.

Milton, Katharine (March 1, 2000). "Hunter-gatherer diets—A different perspective". *The American Journal of Clinical Nutrition* **71** (3): 665–67. PMID 10702155.

Milton, Katharine; Miller, JB; Eaton, SB; Mann, N (1 December 2000). "Reply to L Cordain et al" (PDF). *The American Journal of Clinical Nutrition* **72** (6): 1590–92. PMID 11101497.

Walker, Alexander RP (1 February 2001). "Are health and ill-health lessons from hunter-gatherers currently relevant?". *The American Journal of Clinical Nutrition* **73** (2): 353–56. PMID 11157335.

Mann, NJ; Ponnampalam, EN; Yep, Y; Sinclair, AJ (2003). "Feeding regimes affect fatty acid composition in Australian beef cattle". *Asia Pacific journal of clinical nutrition*. 12 Suppl: S38. PMID 15023647.

Ströhle, A.; Hahn, A.; Sebastian, A. (2010). "Estimation of the diet-dependent net acid load in 229 worldwide historically studied hunter-gatherer societies". *The American journal of clinical nutrition* **91** (2): 406–412. doi:10.3945/ajcn.2009.28637. PMID 20042527.

Prentice, A. M.; Jebb, S. A. (2003). "Fast foods, energy density and obesity: A possible mechanistic link". *Obesity Reviews* **4** (4): 187–94. doi:10.1046/j.1467-789X.2003.00117.x. PMID 14649369.

Bell, Elizabeth A; Castellanos, Victoria H; Pelkman, Christine L; Thorwart, Michelle L; Rolls, Barbara J (1998). "Energy density of foods affects energy intake in normal-weight women". *The American Journal of Clinical Nutrition* **67** (3): 412–20. PMID 9497184.

Drewnowski, Adam; Darmon, Nicole (2005). "The economics of obesity: Dietary energy density and energy cost". *The American Journal of Clinical Nutrition* **82** (1 Suppl): 265S–273S. PMID 16002835.

Ello-Martin, Julia A; Roe, Liane S; Ledikwe, Jenny H; Beach, Amanda M; Rolls, Barbara J (2007). "Dietary energy density in the treatment of obesity: A year-long trial comparing 2 weight-loss diets". *The American Journal of Clinical Nutrition* **85** (6): 1465–77. PMC 2018610. PMID 17556681.

Foster-Powell K, Holt SH, Brand-Miller J (1 July 2002). "International table of glycemic index and glycemic load values: 2002". *The American Journal of Clinical Nutrition* **76** (1): 5–56. PMID 12081815.

Liljeberg Elmståhl H.; & Björck, Inger ME (2001). "Milk as a supplement to mixed meals may elevate postprandial insulinaemia" (PDF). *European journal of clinical nutrition* **55** (11): 994–99. doi:10.1038/sj.ejcn.1601259. PMID 11641749.

Hoyt G, Hickey MS, Cordain L (2005). "Dissociation of the glycaemic and insulinaemic responses to whole and skimmed milk". *British Journal of Nutrition* **93** (2): 175–77. doi:10.1079/BJN20041304. PMID 15788109.

Frassetto LA, Morris RC Jr, Sellmeyer DE, Sebastian A (February 2008). "Adverse effects of sodium chloride on bone in the aging human population resulting from habitual consumption of typical American diets". *Journal of Nutrition* **138** (2): 419S–22S. PMID 18203914.

Remer, T.; Manz, F. (1995). "Potential Renal Acid Load of Foods and its Influence on Urine pH". *Journal of the American Dietetic Association* **95** (7): 791–797. doi:10.1016/S0002-8223(95)00219-7. PMID 7797810.

Frassetto, L. A.; Morris Jr, R. C.; Sebastian, A. (2006). "A practical approach to the balance between acid production and renal acid excretion in humans". *Journal of nephrology*. 19 Suppl 9: S33–S40. PMID 16736439.

Larsen, Clark Spencer (1 November 2003). "Animal source foods and human health during evolution". *Journal of Nutrition* **133** (11, Suppl 2): 3893S–3897S. PMID 14672287.

Hermanussen, Michael; Poustka, Fritz (July–September 2003). "Stature of early Europeans". *Hormones (Athens)* **2** (3): 175–8. doi:10.1159/000079404. PMID 17003019.

Eaton SB, Konner M, Shostak M (April 1988). "Stone agers in the fast lane: chronic degenerative diseases in evolutionary perspective" (PDF). *The American Journal of Medicine* **84** (4): 739–49. doi:10.1016/0002-9343(88)90113-1. PMID 3135745.

Lindeberg S, Eliasson M, Lindahl B, Ahrén B (October 1999). "Low serum insulin in traditional Pacific Islanders—The Kitava study". *Metabolism* **48** (10): 1216–19. doi:10.1016/S0026-0495(99)90258-5. PMID 10535381.

Cannon, Geoffrey (August 2007). "Drugs and bugs, and other stories [Out of the Box]". *Public Health Nutrition* **10** (8): 758–61. doi:10.1017/S1368980007770568.

Leach, Jeff D. (2007). "Paleo Longevity Redux (Letters to the Editor)". *Public Health Nutrition* **10** (11). doi:10.1017/S1368980007814492.

Leonard, William R. (December 2002). "Food for thought: Dietary change was a driving force in human evolution" (PDF). *Scientific American* **287** (6): 106–15. PMID 12469653.

Uauy, Ricardo; & Díaz, Erik (October 2005). "Consequences of food energy excess and positive energy balance". *Public Health Nutrition* **8** (7A): 1077–99. doi:10.1079/PHN2005797. PMID 16277821.

önsson T, Ahrén B, Pacini G, Sundler F, Wierup N, Steen S, Sjöberg T, Ugander M, Frostegård J, Göransson L, Lindeberg S (2006). "A Paleolithic diet confers higher insulin sensitivity, lower C-reactive protein and lower blood pressure than a cereal-based diet in domestic pigs". *Nutrition & Metabolism* **3** (39): 39. doi:10.1186/1743-7075-3-39. PMC 1635051. PMID 17081292.

Jönsson T, Granfeldt Y, Erlanson-Albertsson C, Ahrén B, Lindeberg S (November 2010). "A Paleolithic diet is more satiating per calorie than a Mediterranean-like diet in individuals with ischemic heart disease" (PDF). *Nutr Metab (Lond)* **7** (1): 85. doi:10.1186/1743-7075-7-85. PMC 3009971. PMID 21118562.

Jönsson T, Granfeldt Y, Ahren B, Branell UC, Palsson G, Hansson A, Lindeberg S (2009). "Beneficial effects of a Paleolithic diet on cardiovascular risk factors in type 2 diabetes: a randomized crossover pilot study". *Cardiovascular Diabetology* **8** (1): 35–49. doi:10.1186/1475-2840-8-35. PMC 2724493. PMID 19604407.

Osterdahl M, Kocturk T, Koochek A, Wändell PE (May 2008). "Effects of a short-term intervention with a Paleolithic diet in healthy volunteers". *European Journal of Clinical Nutrition* **62** (5): 682–85. doi:10.1038/sj.ejcn.1602790. PMID 17522610.

Printed in Great Britain
by Amazon.co.uk, Ltd.,
Marston Gate.